Table of contents

1. Introduction 6
2. What is a prompt? 7
   The anatomy of the prompt 7
   Types of prompts 7
3. Why is prompt writing important? 8
   The effects of poor writing prompt design 8
   The benefits of effective prompt writing 8
   Economic impact 8
   Creative and educational impact 8
4. Basic principles for writing good prompts 9
   Clarity as a cornerstone 9
   Specificity as power 9
   Contextual richness 9
   Format specification 9
   Iterative improvement 10
5. Understand ChatGPT's functionality and limitations 11
   How ChatGPT generates responses 11
   Knowledge limitations 11
   Factuality challenges 11
   Contextual constraints 11
   Creative strengths 12
6. How to formulate clear and specific prompts 12
   From vague to specific 12
   Using the WHO-WHAT-WHY framework 12
   Techniques for increased precision 13
   Linguistic precision techniques 13
   Structured prompt templates 13
7. Using context to guide responses 14
   Types of context 14
   How context affects AI's responses 14
   Strategies for effective context usage 15
   Balance context quantity 15

8. Question types and their impact on responses ... 16
Open questions ... 16
Closed questions ... 16
Instructions as questions ... 17
Comparative questions ... 17
Hypothetical questions ... 17
Strategic question combination ... 17
9. Techniques for getting more detailed answers ... 18
Explanation-promoting techniques ... 18
Example and illustration techniques ... 18
Comparative analysis techniques ... 19
In-depth analysis techniques ... 19
Structuring techniques ... 19
Practical application techniques ... 20
10. Use of examples and instructions ... 21
The power of concrete examples ... 21
Style check example ... 21
Format examples for structuring ... 22
Examples for creative guidance ... 22
Instructions for process documentation ... 23
Examples for business communication ... 23
Examples for technical documentation ... 24
Cumulative example strategy ... 24
11. Prompt Design Best Practices ... 25
Systematic prompt development ... 25
Prompt architecture principles ... 25
Quality assurance of prompts ... 25
Prompt chaining for complex tasks ... 26
Iterative improvement ... 26
Efficiency tips ... 26
Ethical considerations in prompt design ... 27

12. Common mistakes to avoid 28
Vagueness and ambiguity 28
Information overload 28
Lack of context 29
Expectations for perfect first results 29
Ignoring AI's limitations 29
Missing format specification 30
Cultural and linguistic assumptions 30
Excessive design of prompts 30
Lack of quality control 30
Inconsistent terminology 30
13. Customizing prompts for different purposes 31
Analytical purposes 31
Creative purposes 31
Educational purposes 32
Business strategic purposes 32
Technical purposes 33
Communicative purposes 33
Decision-making purposes 33
Process improvement purposes 34
14. Writing prompts for creativity and stories 35
Basic principles of creative prompts 35
Storytelling techniques 35
Creative writing techniques 36
Poetic and lyrical prompts 36
Creative description techniques 36
Dialogue and voice 36
Creative constraints that drive innovation 37
Creative collaboration techniques 37
15. Writing prompts for technical and scientific subjects 38
Basic principles of technical prompts 38
Technical documentation structures 38
Scientific explanations 39
Technical problem solving 39

16. Using prompts to generate code and data 40
Structured code request 40
Data processing and analysis 41
Algorithm and data structure 41
17. Creating prompts for business and marketing purposes 42
Strategic content planning 42
Sales and customer engagement 42
Digital marketing 43
18. Using prompts for education and training 44
Pedagogical structuring 44
Adaptive teaching 44
Professional development 45
19. Evaluating and improving prompts 46
Evaluation criteria 46
Iterative improvement 46
Performance optimization 47
20. Prompt Writing Tools and Resources 48
Developer tools 48
Analysis tools 48
Resources and community 48
Specialized tools 49
21. The future of prompt design and AI interaction 50
Technological trends 50
User experience 50
Professional application 51
Ethical considerations 51
22. Case studies and examples 52
Technical documentation 52
Customer service 52
Educational content 53
Creative content production 53

23. Summary and key points 54
Basic principles 54
Strategic application 54
Continuous improvement 54
Future perspectives 54
24. Frequently Asked Questions (FAQ) 55
How long should a prompt be? 55
What do I do if the AI doesn't understand my prompt? 55
How can I get more creative answers? 55
Can I reuse successful prompts? 55
How do I ensure quality in AI-generated content? 55
What are the most common mistakes in prompt design? 56
How do I deal with bias in AI responses? 56
25. Conclusion and further reading 57
Important lessons learned 57
Practical application 57
Skills development 57
Future opportunities 57

Imprint

Title: How to Write Effective Prompts for ChatGPT: A Complete Guide

Author: Karma X

Publisher: BoD · Books on Demand, Östermalmstorg 1, 114 42 Stockholm, Sverige, bod@bod.se
Print: Libri Plureos GmbH, Friedensallee 273, 22763 Hamburg, Tyskland

Year of Publication: 2025

ISBN: 978-91-8097-130-0

1. Introduction

In the digital age, artificial intelligence has become an integral part of our daily lives and work. ChatGPT represents one of the most powerful and accessible AI tools available today, with the capacity to assist in everything from creative writing to technical problem solving.

This comprehensive guide will explore how you can write effective prompts for ChatGPT to maximize results and minimize frustration. Designing good prompts is both an art and a science that combines clarity, precision, and creativity with a deep understanding of how AI systems work.

Whether you are a beginner just starting out with AI tools or an experienced user looking to refine your techniques, this guide will provide you with practical tools and strategies for communicating more effectively with AI. You will learn to understand AI's limitations, leverage its strengths, and develop a systematic approach to prompt design that consistently delivers high-quality results.

By mastering the art of writing effective prompts, you can save valuable time, increase your productivity, and unlock entirely new possibilities for creativity and problem-solving. This guide will take you step-by-step through the entire process, from basic principles to advanced techniques and specialized applications.

2. What is a prompt?

A prompt is the instruction (writing prompt), question, or scenario you give to ChatGPT to generate a response. It acts as a bridge between your human intent and AI's language processing. A prompt can be anything from a simple question like "What is the capital of Sweden?" to a complex instruction that includes context, specific requirements, and examples of desired output.

The anatomy of the prompt

An effective prompt typically consists of several components that work together to guide the AI's response:

Contextual background: This part gives the AI the necessary information to understand the situation. Example: "As an experienced project manager in the IT industry..."

Specific task or question: The central instruction that clearly states what you want the AI to do. Example: "...create a timeline for implementing a new CRM system."

Format and style requirements: Specifies how the response should be structured. Example: "Present this as a weekly timeline with clear milestones."

Limitations and parameters: Defines the framework for the response. Example: "Limit to a maximum of 8 weeks and include risks."

Types of prompts

Informative prompts aim to extract knowledge or explanations from the AI. These are often phrased as direct questions or requests for explanations.

Instructional prompts give the AI specific tasks to perform, such as writing, analyzing, or creating something.

Creative prompts encourage the AI to generate original content, stories, or ideas.

Analytical prompts ask the AI to examine, compare, or evaluate information.

Understanding these basic categories will help you choose the right approach for your specific situation and formulate prompts that lead to desired results.

3. Why is prompt writing important?

The quality of your prompt directly determines the quality of the AI's response. A poorly formulated prompt can lead to unclear, irrelevant, or even misleading results, while a well-constructed prompt can generate insightful, useful, and precise responses that save time and resources.

The effects of poor writing prompt design

When prompts are vague or unclear, several problems can arise. The AI can misinterpret your intent and provide answers that are completely irrelevant to your needs. Lack of context can lead the AI to make incorrect assumptions about what you are looking for. Insufficient specificity often results in generic answers that require extensive follow-up questions.

The benefits of effective prompt writing

Well-designed prompts improve the AI's ability to understand your needs and deliver quality results that are immediately actionable. This saves considerable time by reducing the need for rewording and clarification. Productivity increases when you can get the right information or help on the first try.

Economic impact

For businesses and professional users, the difference between effective and ineffective prompts can translate into tangible financial benefits. Less time spent reformulating questions means more time for value-adding activities. Better quality of AI-generated content reduces the need for extensive editing and quality control.

Creative and educational impact

In creative and educational contexts, effective prompts enable deeper exploration of ideas and concepts. AI can become a more powerful brainstorming partner when it understands exactly what kind of creative input you are looking for. In educational contexts, well-crafted prompts can help create more engaging and relevant learning experiences.

4. Basic principles for writing good prompts

Writing effective prompts is based on several fundamental principles that, when applied consistently, dramatically improve the quality of AI responses.

Clarity as a cornerstone

Clarity is the most fundamental element of prompt design. Every word in your prompt should serve a purpose and help communicate your intent. Avoid unnecessary words or phrases that can confuse or detract from the core instruction.

When formulating your prompt, read it aloud to yourself and ask yourself if the meaning is clear to someone who does not have your background knowledge. If you experience any doubt about how prompts should be interpreted, the AI will have the same problem.

Specificity as power

Specific prompts generate specific answers. Instead of asking "Tell me about marketing," you should phrase it like "Explain the three most important differences between digital marketing and traditional marketing for small businesses in the retail industry."

Specificity is not just about subject matter, but also about scope, depth, and perspective. The more precise you can be about what you want, the better the AI can deliver.

Contextual richness

Context is the information that helps the AI understand not only what you are asking but why you are asking it. This understanding enables more relevant and useful answers.

Include relevant background information such as your role, industry, or situation. If you are a student, this may affect how the technical information should be presented. If you work in a specific sector, industry-specific examples may be more valuable.

Format specification

The AI can produce information in many different formats, from bullet lists to detailed essays, from code examples to poetic descriptions. By specifying the desired format, you get information that is immediately useful for your purpose.

Usual format specifications include length (number of words or characters), structure (bullet list, numbered list paragraphs), style (formal, informal, technical), and presentation (tables, diagrams, step-by-step instructions).

Iterative improvement

Prompt writing is an iterative process. Your first prompt will rarely be perfect, and it is perfectly normal to need to adjust and refine based on the responses you get.

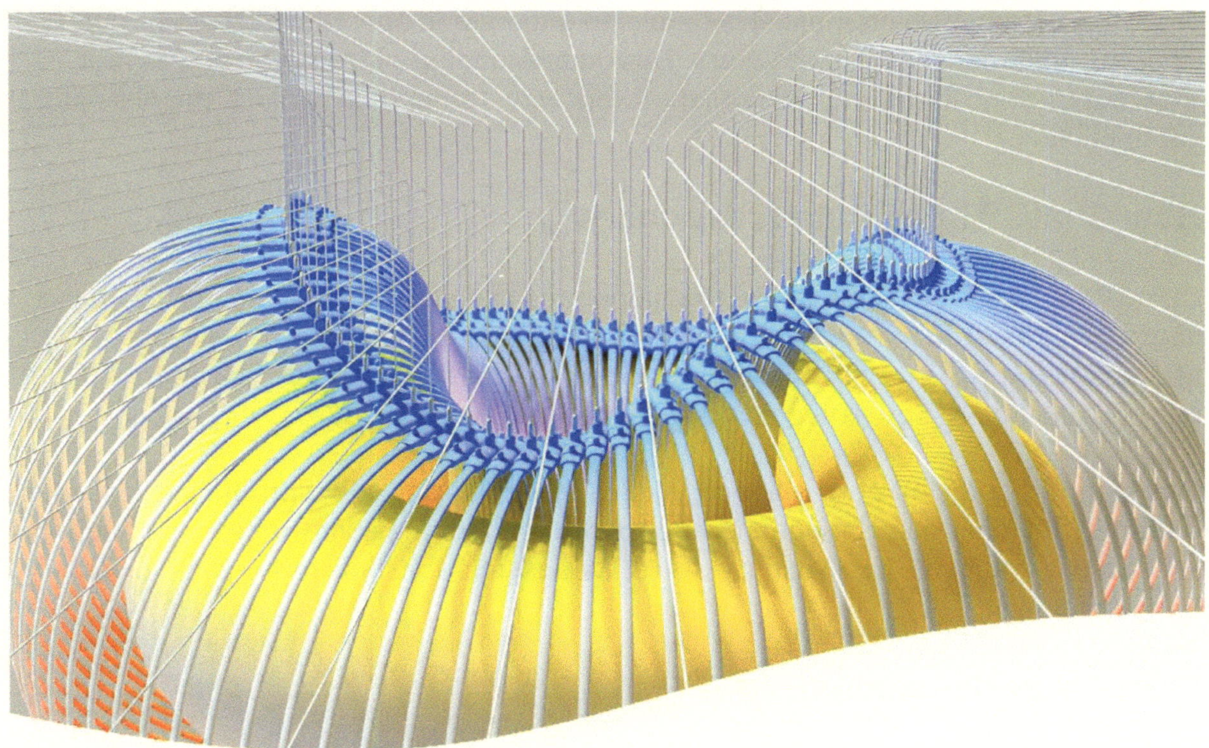

Document which prompts work well for several types of tasks. This creates a personal library of effective prompt templates that you can use and customize for future needs.

5. Understand ChatGPT's functionality and limitations

To write truly effective prompts, it is crucial to understand how ChatGPT works and what the limitations of the system are. This understanding will help you adjust your expectations and formulate prompts that work with, rather than against, the AI's natural capabilities.

How ChatGPT generates responses

ChatGPT is a large language model that generates text by predicting the next word in a sequence, based on massive amounts of training data. It does not have awareness or understanding in the traditional sense but identifies patterns in language and reproduces them in sophisticated ways.

This means that the AI is exceptionally skilled at recognizing and reproducing linguistic patterns, but it has no real understanding of the world or the ability to reason in the same way as humans. It works based on statistical relationships rather than logical understanding.

Knowledge limitations

ChatGPT's knowledge is limited to the information available at the time of entry, with a specific end date. It cannot access real-time information or dynamically update its knowledge base.

This means that up-to-date information about events, new products, or the latest research findings may not be available. When you need highly up-to-date information, you should supplement the AI's responses with verification from reliable, up-to-date sources.

Factuality challenges

AI can sometimes generate information that sounds convincing but is incorrect. This phenomenon is called "hallucination" and occurs when AI fills in knowledge gaps with plausible sounding but incorrect information.

To deal with this, you should develop a healthy skepticism towards AI responses, especially for factual claims. Verification from trusted sources is important, especially for information that will be used in professional or academic contexts.

Contextual constraints

ChatGPT has limitations in how much context it can hold in memory at once. Extraordinarily long conversations can lead to previous information being "forgotten", which can affect the consistency of responses.

For complex projects that require continuity across multiple interactions, it can be beneficial to regularly summarize previous discussion or break down large tasks into smaller, more manageable parts.

Creative strengths

Despite its limitations, AI is exceptionally strong in creative applications. It can generate ideas, write creative content, and assist with brainstorming in ways that can be unbelievably valuable.

AI's ability to combine concepts in unexpected ways and generate copious amounts of variation on themes makes it a powerful tool for creative inspiration and development.

6. How to formulate clear and specific prompts

Formulating clear and specific prompts is a fundamental skill that separates effective AI users from those who struggle with unsatisfactory results. This section provides you with practical techniques for transforming vague ideas into precise instructions.

From vague to specific

Let us examine the transformation from vague to specific prompts through concrete examples:

Vague prompt: "Help me with my resume." **Specific prompt:** "Review my resume for a product manager position in technology and provide three concrete suggestions for improvement to highlight my experience with agile development and user-centered design."

Vague prompt: “Write about marketing.” **Specific prompt:** “Create an 800-word article on how small businesses in the restaurant industry can use social media to increase customer loyalty, focusing on Instagram and Facebook strategies.”

Using the WHO-WHAT-WHY framework

An effective way to structure specific prompts is to use the WHO-WHAT-WHY framework:

WHO defines the target audience or perspective: "As a beginner in programming..." **WHAT** specifies exactly what to do: "...create a step-by-step guide to building a simple web page..." **WHY** explains the purpose or context: "...to demonstrate basic HTML and CSS skills in a portfolio."

Techniques for increased precision

Quantification: Use specific metrics whenever possible. Instead of "write a short article," say "write a 500-word article."

Exemplification: Include examples of what you are looking for. "Write headlines like 'Five Ways to Increase Productivity' or 'Why Small Businesses Benefit from Personal Service.'"

Parameterization: Define clear boundaries and requirements. "Limit the answer to three main points, use a formal tone, include sources where possible."

Linguistic precision techniques

Active voice: Use active voice for clearer instructions. Instead of "The content should be written," use "Write the content."

Concrete verbs: Choose specific action verbs. Instead of "manage," use "analyze," "summarize," or "compare."

Eliminate ambiguity: Avoid words that can be interpreted in multiple ways. Instead of "several," use "three to five" or other specific quantification.

Structured prompt templates

Develop templates for common task types:

Analysis template: "Analyze [topic] from the perspective of [role/industry]. Focus on [specific aspects]. Present the results as [format] and include [specific elements]."

Creative template: "Create [type of content] for [target audience] with [specific objective]. The tone should be [description], and the content should include [specific elements]."

Problem-solving template: "I am faced with [specific problem] within [context]. Provide [number] practical solutions that consider [constraints/requirements]. Prioritize solutions according to [criteria]."

7. Using context to guide responses

Context is the secret ingredient that transforms generic AI responses into tailored, relevant content. By skillfully using context, you can direct the AI to generate responses that are perfectly tailored to your specific situation, audience, and purpose.

Types of context

Personal context includes information about your role, industry, experience level, and specific situation. "As a newbie in digital marketing working for a B2B company in the software industry..."

Situational context describes the circumstances under which the information will be used. "For a presentation to management next week..."

The audience context specifies who will consume the generated content. "For an article aimed at small business owners without a technical background..."

Industry context provides AI with information about specific industries, regulations, or standards that are relevant. "In the financial industry where GDPR compliance is critical..."

How context affects AI's responses

Context acts as a lens through which the AI filters and adapts its responses. The same technical information can be presented very differently depending on whether the recipient is an expert or a novice, whether the purpose is education or problem-solving, or whether the context is formal or informal.

Example without context: Prompt: "Explain blockchain." Answer: [Generic technical explanation]

Example with context: Prompt: "As the CEO of a traditional bank considering blockchain implementation, explain blockchain technology to my non-technical board, focusing on the business benefits and risks." Answer: [Custom answer with business focus, non-technical language, relevant to the banking industry]

Strategies for effective context usage

Role definition: Start your prompt by defining the perspective. "As an experienced HR specialist..." or "From the perspective of an environmentally conscious consumer..."

Scenario building: Create a clear picture of the situation. "While preparing for a product launch where we have a limited budget and need to maximize ROI..."

Restriction Specification: Include relevant restrictions or requirements. "In light of GDPR requirements and company data security policy..."

Target audience: Clearly define who the information is for. "For a workshop for middle managers who are comfortable with basic business analysis but not with advanced statistics..."

Balance context quantity

Too much context can overload prompts and make them difficult to follow, while too little context results in generic responses. The optimal amount of context includes all the information necessary to guide the response without including irrelevant details.

A useful rule is to include context that directly affects how the response should be phrased, structured, or focused. If the context does not change how the AI should respond, it is unnecessary.

8. Question types and their impact on responses

Several types of questions generate fundamentally diverse types of responses from AI. By understanding how question wording affects response style and content, you can strategically choose question type based on what you want to achieve.

Open questions

Open-ended questions typically begin with "what," "how," "why," or "describe" and encourage detailed, elaborate answers. These questions are ideal when you want in-depth explanations, creative ideas, or extensive analysis.

Examples of open questions:

- "What are the long-term consequences of remote work for company culture?"
- "How can small businesses best use AI to improve customer service?"
- "Why is user experience crucial to e-commerce success?"

Open-ended questions tend to generate responses that are rich in detail, contain multiple perspectives, and often include examples and explanations. They are especially useful for exploring complex topics where you want to understand the nuances.

Closed questions

Closed questions can be answered with "yes," "no," or short, specific information. They are effective when you need quick, direct answers or when you want to confirm specific information.

Examples of close questions:

- "Is Python suitable for web application development?"
- "What year was Google founded?"
- "Can GDPR affect US businesses?"

While closed questions elicit short answers, you can often combine them with more open-ended follow-ups to get both confirmation and depth.

Instructions as questions

Instructions phrased as prompts rather than questions give you more control over the format and structure of your response. These are ideal when you know exactly what you want and how they should be presented.

Example instructions:

- "List five strategies for improving team communication."
- "Create a weekly workout plan for beginners."
- "Summarize the main points from the attached article."

Comparative questions

Comparative questions ask the AI to analyze differences and similarities between alternatives. These are valuable for decision-making and understanding the relative advantages and disadvantages.

Examples of comparative questions:

- "Compare the advantages and disadvantages of cloud computing versus local servers for small businesses."
- "What are the differences between agile and waterfall project management?"

Hypothetical questions

Hypothetical questions explore "what if" scenarios and are useful for planning, risk analysis, and creative problem solving.

Examples of hypothetical questions:

- "What would happen if our company lost its largest customer?"
- "How would the market react if new technology made our products obsolete?"

Strategic question combination

Often the most effective approach is to combine different question types in a sequence that builds from general understanding to specific application:

1. Start with an open-ended question to establish basic understanding
2. Follow up with comparative questions to understand alternatives
3. Using instructions to get specific, useful results
4. End with hypothetical questions for future planning

9. Techniques for getting more detailed answers

Getting deep, insightful answers from AI requires specific techniques that encourage elaboration and detail. These methods help you go beyond superficial answers and get the kind of comprehensive information that truly adds value.

Explanation-promoting techniques

Ask for step-by-step explanations: When you want to understand a process or procedure, ask the AI to break it down into clear, sequential steps.

Example: "Explain the process of launching a new product, step by step, from initial idea to market introduction."

Use "why" questions: These encourage deeper analysis of causes and consequences.

Example: "Why is customer loyalty more important for subscription services than for traditional retail?"

Ask for justification: Encourage the AI to explain the reasoning behind recommendations or claims.

Example: "Recommend three project management tools for small businesses and explain why each is suitable for different types of organizations."

Example and illustration techniques

Ask for concrete examples: Abstract concepts become more understandable with practical illustrations.

Example: "Explain the concept of 'viral marketing' and give three specific examples of successful viral campaigns from recent years."

Request case studies: These provide in-depth insights into how theories are applied in practice.

Example: "Analyze how a successful company has implemented sustainability initiatives and what results they achieved."

Ask for scenarios: Hypothetical situations help illustrate how principles apply under different circumstances.

Comparative analysis techniques

Ask for pros and cons: These provide balanced perspectives on decisions or alternatives.

Example: "List the advantages and disadvantages of using freelancers versus permanent employees for creative projects."

Request comparative tables: Structured comparisons make it easier to evaluate alternatives.

Example: "Create a comparison table showing the features, costs, and uses of the three most popular CRM systems."

In-depth analysis techniques

Ask for multi-perspective analysis: Encourage the AI to look at the topic from different angles.

Example: "Analyze the effects of remote work from the perspectives of employees, employers, and society as a whole."

Request trend and future analysis: Explore not only the current state but also likely developments.

Example: "Describe current trends in e-commerce and predict how the industry might develop over the next five years."

Structuring techniques

Use numerical constraints: Specify the number of points to ensure sufficient coverage without overwhelming the response.

Example: "Provide five detailed strategies for improving employee engagement, with an explanation of implementation and expected results for each."

Ask for hierarchical structuring: This helps organize complex information.

Example: "Organize the most important skills for a digital marketer into categories from basic to advanced, with explanations for each level."

Practical application techniques

Ask for implementation guides: Transform theoretical knowledge into practical action plans.

Example: "Create a 30-day implementation plan to improve an e-commerce website's SEO, with specific tasks for each week."

Request resource lists: Supplement information with tools and resources for continued learning or implementation.

Example: "Explain content marketing for B2B companies and include recommended tools, resources, and measurement methods."

10. Use of examples and instructions

Examples are one of the most powerful techniques for controlling AI output. By showing the AI exactly what you want, rather than just describing it, you can dramatically improve the relevance and quality of the responses generated.

The power of concrete examples

Examples function as templates that the AI can follow and adapt. They eliminate guesswork and provide clear guidance on style, format, depth, and approach. This is especially valuable when working with creative content, technical documentation, or specific business formats.

Without example: "Write product descriptions for our e-commerce site."

For example: "Write product descriptions for our e-commerce site. Here is an example of the style we want: 'This handmade ceramic mug turns your morning coffee into a ritual of indulgence. With its ergonomic design and heat-retaining properties, it keeps your drink at the perfect temperature, while the rustic finish adds a touch of elegance to your kitchen. Perfect for the coffee connoisseur who values both function and style.'"

Style check example

Formal business tone: "Use a professional, formal tone as in this example: 'We are pleased to announce the implementation of our new quality assurance system, which will improve both efficiency and customer satisfaction according to expected timeframes.'"

Informal, friendly tone: "Write in a casual, personal style like this: 'Hey there! We just launched something really cool that will make your life easier. “Want to know more?'"

Technical precision: "Use precise, technical language, as in this example: 'The system implements OAuth 2.0 authentication with 256-bit SSL encryption for secure data transmission and uses RESTful API architecture for optimal scalability.'"

Format examples for structuring

Lists and bullet points: "Structure the information like this example: Main point with short explanation

- Supporting detail
- Additional specification • Next main point
- Related information"

Table format: "Present the comparison in table format according to this example:

Function	Product A	Product B	Recommendation
Price	$299	$399	Product A for budget
Performance	Means	High	Product B for professional use

Step-by-step format: "Follow this structure for instructions: Step 1: [Action] - [Explanation of why this step is important] Step 2: [Next action] - [Result you expect] Step 3: [Continuation] - [Troubleshooting tips]"

Examples for creative guidance

Narrative style: "Write in the same narrative style as this example: 'Maria looked at her first AI-generated artwork with mixed emotions. The algorithms had captured something she could never put into words - a sense of longing that permeated every pixel. This was the beginning of her journey from skeptic to advocate of AI art.'"

Descriptive Language: "Use rich, descriptive language as in this example: 'The golden sunset cast long shadows across the bustling marketplace, where the scent of fresh spices mingled with the sounds of lively bargaining and laughter from passing families.'"

Instructions for process documentation

Detailed process documentation: "Document the process according to this template:

Process name: [Clear, descriptive title]

Objective: [What to achieve]

Prerequisites: [What is needed before the process starts]

Step:

1. [Specific action with details]
2. [Next action with expected results]
3. [Continuation of quality checks]

Quality control: [How do you verify that the result is correct]

Common Problems: [Potential Challenges and Solutions]"

Examples for business communication

Project Updates: "Follow this structure for project reports:

Project status: [Green/Yellow/Red with brief explanation]

Activities conducted during this period:

- [Specific activity] - [Completed date]
- [Other activity] - [Status and next steps]

Upcoming milestones:

- [Milestone] - [Planned date] - [Responsible person]

Risks and challenges:

- [Risk] - [Probability] - [Proposed Action]

Resource requirements:

- [Type of resource] - [When] - [Why]"

Examples for technical documentation

API documentation: "Document endpoints according to this format:

Endpoint: GET /api/v1/users/{id}

Description: Retrieves detailed user information based on user ID

Parameters:

- id (required, integer): Unique user ID
- include_metadata (optional, boolean): Includes metadata in the response

Example answer:

```
{
"user_id": 12345,
"name": "Anna Andersson",
"email": "anna@example.com",
"created_at": "2023-01-15T10:30:00Z"
}
```

Error handling:

- 404: User not found
- 401: Unauthorized Access"

Cumulative example strategy

An advanced technique is to use multiple examples that show variation within the same style or format. This gives the AI greater flexibility while maintaining consistency.

"Write product reviews in the same style as these examples:

Example 1: 'This tool exceeded all my expectations. As someone who has used related products for over five years, I can say that the quality is exceptional, and the performance is dependable even under intensive use.'

Example 2: 'First impressions were positive, but after a few months of use I noticed some limitations. For basic needs it works great, but professional users may want to consider more expensive options.'

Example 3: 'Easy to use right out of the box, which is rare for this type of product. The instructions were clear, and customer service was helpful when I had questions.'"

11. Prompt Design Best Practices

Developing consistent, effective prompt design routines requires a systematic approach and understanding of what works overtime. This section compiles proven methods that professional AI users have developed through experience.

Systematic prompt development

Start broad, narrow incrementally: Start with a basic prompt and refine it iteratively based on results. This avoids overcomplicating from the start and allows you to identify which elements really impact quality.

Document successful patterns: Keep a library of prompts that work well for several types of tasks. Categorize them by purpose (creative, analytical, technical) and note what makes them effective.

Assess systematically: When developing a key prompt, create multiple variations and compare the results. Document on which changes lead to improvements.

Prompt architecture principles

Hierarchical information structure: Organize your prompt logically with the most important instructions first, followed by context, and then specific requirements or constraints.

Examples of good structure:

1. Primary instruction (what to do)
2. Context and background (why and for whom)
3. Format and style requirements (how it should be presented)
4. Specific limitations or parameters

Clear delimitation: Use delimiters to separate various parts of complex prompts. This can be indents, numbering, or special markings.

Quality assurance of prompts

Readability test: Read your prompt aloud to yourself. If you must pause to understand what you mean, the AI is having the same problem.

Perspective Test: Imagine being given this prompt with no background knowledge. Are the instructions clear enough for someone else to follow?

Specificity Check: Review each adjective and adverb in your prompt. Can they be interpreted in multiple ways? Replace vague descriptions with specific metrics or examples.

Prompt chaining for complex tasks

For complex projects that require multiple steps or several types of output, prompt chaining can be amazingly effective. This involves breaking up large tasks into smaller, focused prompts that build on each other.

Basic chaining structure:

1. Information gathering: "Analyze the following situation and identify key factors..."
2. Alternative generation: "Based on the analysis above, suggest three possible solutions..."
3. Evaluation: "Compare the proposed solutions according to the following criteria..."
4. Implementation: "Create a detailed action plan for the most appropriate solution..."

Iterative improvement

A/B testing of prompts: For important, recurring tasks, develop two versions of the same prompt and compare the results over time.

Results Analysis: After using a prompt, critically evaluate the results. What was good? What was missing? How can prompts be improved next time?

Continuous calibration: AI models update over time, so prompts that worked well in the past may need to be adjusted. Regularly review and update your most used prompts.

Efficiency tips

Template library: Develop reusable templates for common task types. This saves time and ensures consistency.

Standardized formats: For teams or organizations, develop standardized prompt formats that everyone can use. This improves consistency and facilitates knowledge sharing.

Tool integration: Consider using tools that can store and organize your prompts for easy access and reuse.

Ethical considerations in prompt design

Bias awareness: Be aware that prompts can introduce or reinforce bias. Review your prompts for language that could lead to biased or discriminatory responses.

Inclusivity: Formulate prompts in ways that do not exclude or marginalize certain groups. Use inclusive language and consider different perspectives.

Transparency: When AI-generated content is used in professional contexts, ensure there is appropriate transparency about the use of AI tools.

12. Common mistakes to avoid

Understanding and avoiding common prompt writing pitfalls can save you considerable time and frustration. This section identifies the most frequent mistakes and provides concrete strategies for avoiding them.

Vagueness and ambiguity

Mistake: Using vague descriptions like "good," "professional," or "interesting" without defining what this means in your context.

Example of a problematic prompt: "Write a good article about marketing."

Improved version: "Write a 1000-word article on social media strategies for restaurants, aimed at small business owners without marketing training, focusing on practical, implementable advice and concrete examples."

Solution Strategy: Replace all subjective descriptions with objective measures or detailed descriptions. Ask yourself "What exactly do I mean by this word?"

Information overload

Mistake: Packing too much information into a single prompt, making it difficult for the AI to prioritize and focus.

Example of a problematic prompt: "Analyze our company's market position, competitive analysis, customer demographics, product development strategy, financial performance, and future plans for the next quarter while taking into account macroeconomic factors and industry trends."

Improved approach: Split into multiple focused prompts:

1. "Analyze our company's market position compared to three main competitors"
2. "Evaluate our current customer demographics and identify growth opportunities"
3. "Assess how macroeconomic factors will affect our industry next quarter"

Solution Strategy: Use the “one prompt, one focus” principle. If your prompt contains more than three main points, consider breaking it up.

Lack of context

Mistake: If the AI understands your specific situation without providing the necessary background information.

Example of a problematic prompt: "How should we solve our customer support problem?"

Improved version: "Our SaaS company, with 500 customers is experiencing long response times (average 48 hours) in customer support via email. We have two part-time support staff and a limited budget. Suggest three cost-effective solutions to improve response times to under 12 hours."

Solution strategy: Always include relevant background that influences how the problem should be approached or solved.

Expectations for perfect first results

Mistake: Expecting the first prompt to produce perfect results without iteration (improvement cycles) or refinement.

Solution Strategy: View prompt writing as an iterative (continuous) process. Plan for the need to refine and adjust based on initial results.

Ignoring AI's limitations

Mistake: Asking the AI for real-time information, individual opinions, or to do things that are beyond its capabilities.

Examples of problematic requests:

- "What do you think about this strategy?"
- "What happened on the stock market today?"
- "Call this customer and follow up"

Solution Strategy: Understand what AI can and cannot do. Focus on analytics, content generation, information structuring, and creative assistance based on available information.

Missing format specification

Mistake: Not specifying how the results should be structured or presented.

Example of a problematic prompt: "Tell me about project management."

Improved version: "Create a comparison table of the advantages and disadvantages of Agile versus Waterfall project management, focusing on small businesses. Include columns for cost, time, flexibility, and appropriate project types."

Cultural and linguistic assumptions

Mistake: Assuming specific cultural references or linguistic nuances without specifying them.

Solution strategy: Be explicit about cultural context, target audience, and language requirements. Specify whether you want an American or European perspective, formal or informal tone.

Excessive design of prompts

Mistake: Making unnecessarily complex prompts with too many instructions, restrictions, and specifications.

Solution strategy: Start simple and add complexity only when necessary. Evaluate whether a simpler version gives good enough results before adding more instructions.

Lack of quality control

Mistake: Using AI-generated content without verifying or reviewing it.

Solution Strategy: Develop quality control procedures, especially for factual claims, technical information, and professional content. Use AI as a starting point, not an end point.

Inconsistent terminology

Mistake: Using different terms for the same concept within the same prompt or project.

Solution Strategy: Establish and stick to consistent terminology, especially for technical terms or industry-specific concepts.

13. Customizing prompts for different purposes

Different purposes require fundamentally different approaches to prompt design. Understanding how to adapt your communication style and structure based on the desired outcome is crucial to maximizing AI's effectiveness in different contexts.

Analytical purposes

When the goal is in-depth analysis or problem solving, focus on structure, logic, and systematic review.

Analytical prompt structure: "Analyze [topic/situation] by:

1. Identify key factors and their relationships
2. Assess the impact of each factor
3. Draw conclusions based on the evidence
4. Suggest courses of action based on the analysis"

Example: "Analyze why our company's customer satisfaction has decreased by 15% in the last quarter. Review the following Data Point: [specific data], identify possible causes, assess the likelihood of each cause, and propose concrete actions for improvement."

Creative purposes

Creative prompts should provide freedom while also providing direction. Balance inspiration with structure.

Creative prompt structure: "Create [type of content] that [specific goal] by:

- Explore [theme/concept] from [perspective]
- Include elements of [specific components]
- Target [target audience] with [tonality]"

Example: "Create a 500-word story that illustrates the importance of teamwork in a future workplace. Include technological elements such as AI assistants and virtual collaboration, targeting young professionals with an optimistic but realistic tone."

Educational purposes

Pedagogical prompts should focus on clarity, progression, and understanding.

Educational prompt structure: "Explain [concept] to [target audience] by:

1. Start with basic definition
2. Use analogies or examples that are relevant to the target audience
3. Build complexity gradually
4. Include practical applications
5. Conclude with ways to deepen knowledge"

Example: "Explain blockchain technology to small business owners without a technical background. Start with simple analogies, explain how it impacts business operations, provide concrete examples from different industries, and suggest resources for further learning."

Business strategic purposes

Business-oriented prompts should be results-focused and actionable.

Business Strategy Prompt Structure: "Develop [type of strategy] for [business context] that:

- Considering [specific constraints/resources]
- Achieving [measurable goals]
- Includes timeline for implementation
- Addresses potential risks and countermeasures"

Example: "Develop a 6-month digital marketing strategy for our B2B consulting firm with a budget of 50,000 SEK/month. Focus on lead generation with a goal of 20% increase in qualified leads. Include specific channels, content strategy, and KPIs for follow-up."

Technical purposes

Technical prompts require precision, specificity, and structured presentation.

Technical prompt structure: "[Technical task] with the following specifications:

- Technical requirements: [specific parameters]
- Limitations: [technical or resource limits]
- Output format: [exact specification]
- Quality criteria: [testable standards]"

Example: "Create a Python function that validates email addresses according to the RFC 5322 standard. The function should oversee international characters, return boolean values, and include error handling for common exceptional cases. Include documentation and examples of usage."

Communicative purposes

When the purpose is to improve communication or create communication materials, focus on the target audience and message.

Communicative prompt structure: "Create [type of communication] for [specific target audience] that:

- Communicates [main message] clearly
- Uses [appropriate tone and style]
- Achieves [specific communication goal]
- Considers [cultural/contextual factors]"

Decision-making purposes

For decision support, structure prompts to present options and consequences clearly.

Decision-making prompt structure: "Evaluate [decision situation] by:

1. Define all relevant options
2. Identify evaluation criteria
3. Assess each alternative against the criteria
4. Present recommendation with justification
5. Identify risks and limitations"

Process improvement purposes

For process optimization, focus on the current state, desired state, and the path in between.

Process improvement prompt structure: "Analyze [current process] and suggest improvements such as:

- Identifies inefficiencies and bottlenecks
- Proposing concrete improvement measures
- Estimates the impact on [relevant metrics]
- Includes implementation plan
- Addresses potential resistance and challenges"

By tailoring your prompt structure to the specific purpose, you ensure that the AI understands not only what you want, but also how the information should be used and presented.

14. Writing prompts for creativity and stories

Creative prompts require a balance between structure and freedom. Too much constraint kills creativity, while too little direction results in generic or irrelevant results. This section explores techniques for unlocking the creative potential of AI.

Basic principles of creative prompts

Balance constraints with freedom: Provide enough framework to guide creativity without stifling it. Specify genre, length, and basic parameters, but leave room for surprises.

Use sensory details: Encourage the use of all senses to create more vivid and engaging content.

Specify emotional tone: Define the emotional atmosphere you want to achieve, but let the AI choose how it is achieved.

Storytelling techniques

Character-Driven Storytelling: "Create a short story centered around a [type of character] who is confronted with [type of conflict]. The character should have a distinct [personality trait] that both helps and hinders them. The story should take place in [time period/setting] and explore the theme of [abstract concept]."

Situation-driven storytelling: "Write a story that begins with the following situation: [specific starting point]. Explore how different characters react to this situation and how their choices shape the development of the story. Focus on [specific theme] and use [narrative style]."

Atmospheric Story: "Create a story that captures the feeling of [specific atmosphere/mood]. Use environmental descriptions, weather, and sensory details to enhance this atmosphere. Let the mood drive the plot forward."

Creative writing techniques

Stream-of-consciousness prompts: "Write an internal monologue from the perspective of [character] during [specific situation]. Let thoughts flow naturally between the present, memories, and plans. Focus on [emotion or theme]."

Experimental formats: "Tell the same story from three different perspectives: [perspective 1], [perspective 2], and [perspective 3]. Each version should be a maximum of 200 words and reveal different aspects of the truth."

Genre Mix: "Combine elements from [genre 1] and [genre 2] to create a unique story. Use [recurring patterns from both genres] but go against the reader's expectations through [specific twist]."

Poetic and lyrical prompts

Theme-Based Poetry: "Write a poem that explores [abstract concept] through concrete, everyday imagery. Use [poetic form] and focus on [sensory experience]. Let each stanza build on the previous one to create emotional progression."

Narrative Poetry: "Create a narrative poem that follows [character] through [event sequence]. Use rhythm and rhyme to reinforce the momentum of the story. Include dialogue and descriptive passages that drive the plot forward."

Creative description techniques

Setting Description: "Describe [location/environment] in a way that reveals the character observing it. Use details that reflect [character's mood/background]. Make the setting almost a character in itself."

Character Portrait: "Create a vivid portrait of [type of character] without directly describing their appearance. Instead, use their actions, speech patterns, choices, and reactions to reveal who they are. Focus on [specific aspect of personality]."

Dialogue and voice

Distinctive voice: "Write a dialogue between [character 1] and [character 2] where each character's personality comes through clearly in their way of speaking. [Character 1] should use [language style/pattern] while [character 2] uses [different language style]. The conversation should reveal [specific information] without anyone directly saying it."

Subtext Dialogue: "Create a conversation where the characters say one thing but mean something completely different. The subtext should be about [hidden theme] while the surface discusses [everyday topic]. Let the reader understand the real meaning through context and the characters' reactions."

Creative constraints that drive innovation

Formal constraints: "Write a story of exactly 55 words that tells a complete story with a beginning, middle, and end. Every word must serve a purpose."

Language limitations: "Create a story without using adjectives. Let nouns and verbs carry all the descriptive burden."

Conceptual constraints: "Write a love story where the word 'love' is never used. Show the feeling through actions, symbols, and dialogue."

Creative collaboration techniques

Collaborative Creativity: "Start a story with the following first sentence: [given sentence]. Write the next 200 words and end with a cliffhanger that sets up a surprising twist."

Improvisational Writing: "Take these three random elements: [element 1], [element 2], [element 3] and weave them into a coherent story in a natural way. Let the elements inspire plot development rather than just being interspersed in detail."

Creative prompts require experimentation and risk-taking. Do not be afraid of unconventional combinations or odd constraints - these often lead to the most original and memorable results.

15. Writing prompts for technical and scientific subjects

Technical and scientific prompts require precision, accuracy, and structured communication. These prompts must balance complexity with clarity and ensure that technical information is communicated at an appropriate level for the target audience.

Basic principles of technical prompts

Precision specification: Technical terms have specific meanings that cannot be approximated. Be precise in your terminology and specify which definition or standard you are referring to.

Complexity level definition: Clearly define the technical level of the target audience. An explanation for an expert is dramatically different from one for a beginner.

Contextual information: Technical information does not exist in a vacuum. Always specify the technical context and scope.

Technical documentation structures

API Documentation: "Create complete documentation for the following API endpoint:

- Endpoint URL and HTTP method
- Description of functionality
- Required and optional parameters with data types
- Example of request and response
- Error codes and their meanings
- Authentication requirements
- Rate limiting information (limiting data)"

System architecture description: "Describe [system/architecture] with a focus on:

- Overall system overview and main components
- Data flow between components
- Technical choices and justifications
- Scalability and performance requirements
- Safety considerations
- Dependencies and external integrations"

Scientific explanations

Research summary: "Summarize the following scientific study for [target audience]:

- Research question and hypothesis
- Methodology and data basis
- Main results and statistical significance
- Limitations and methodological considerations
- Implications for practical application
- Suggestions for future research"

Theoretical concept explanation: "Explain [scientific concept] at [level] with:

- Basic definition and principles
- Historical development and key researchers
- Mathematical or physical relationships
- Practical applications and examples
- Common misunderstandings and errors
- Relationship to closely related concepts"

Technical problem solving

Troubleshooting Guide: "Create systematic troubleshooting guide for [problem]:

- Problem identification and symptoms
- Step-by-step diagnostics
- Common causes and their solutions
- Troubleshooting tools and resources
- Preventive measures
- When professional help is needed"

Design specification: "Develop technical specification for [system/component]:

- Functional requirements and limitations
- Technical specifications and standards
- Performance requirements and measurement criteria
- Safety and security requirements
- Compatibility and integration requirements
- Evaluate criteria and quality assurance"

16. Using prompts to generate code and data

Code generation through prompts requires structured communication about technical requirements, programming standards, and functional specifications. Effective code prompts balance specificity with flexibility to produce usable and maintainable code.

Structured code request

Function specification: "Create a [programming language] function that:

- Accepts the following parameters: [specify types and purpose]
- Perform the following operations: [detailed description]
- Returns: [type and format of output]
- Manages the following errors: [error types and handling strategy]
- Follows [code standard/style guide]
- Includes documentation and comments"

Class Design: "Design a [programming language] class for [purpose]:

- Attributes and their data types
- Constructor with initialization
- Public and private methods
- Encapsulation and data validation
- Inheritance or composition if relevant
- Unit tests for main functionality"

Data processing and analysis

Data analysis script: "Create a data analysis script that:

- Reading data from [source and format]
- Perform data validation and cleansing
- Calculates [specific statistics/metrics]
- Creates [types of visualizations]
- Exporting results to [format]
- Includes error handling for corrupt data"

Database Integration: "Develop code for database interaction such as:

- Connecting to [database type] using secure authentication
- Implements CRUD operations for [entities]
- Applies parameterized search queries for increased security
- Manages connection errors and retries
- Logs transactions for auditing
- Optimizes performance for large data sets"

Algorithm and data structure

Algorithm implementation: "Implement [algorithm] as:

- Solves [specific problem] effectively
- Has time complexity O([complexity])
- Handles [edge cases and exceptional cases]
- Includes step-by-step commentary
- Demonstrated with [number] test cases
- Compared to alternative approaches"

Data Structure Design: "Create a custom data structure for [use]:

- Implements [specific operations]
- Optimizing for [performance/memory requirements]
- Maintains [invariants/properties]
- Supports [iteration/traversal]
- Includes data integrity validation
- "Documents complexity for all operations"

17. Creating prompts for business and marketing purposes

Business and marketing prompts focus on generating content that drives business results, builds brand, and engages audiences. These prompts must balance creativity with strategic focus and measurable goals.

Strategic content planning

Marketing Strategy: "Develop a comprehensive marketing strategy for [product/service]:

- Target audience analysis and persona definition
- Positioning against competitors
- Budget distribution between channels
- Content calendar for [time]
- KPIs and measurement methods
- Risk analysis and contingency plans"

Brand Communication: "Create Brand Guidelines for [Company/Product]:"

- Brand personality and value proposition
- Tone and style of communication
- Visual identity and design principles
- Messages for different target groups
- Social media guidelines
- Crisis management communication"

Sales and customer engagement

Sales process: "Design a sales process for [product/industry]:

- Lead qualification and scoring criteria
- Sales call structure and key questions
- Objection handling for common obstacles
- Follow-up sequences and timing
- CRM integration and tracking
- Sales materials and supporting documents"

Customer retention: "Develop a customer retention strategy that:

- Identifies risk indicators for customer churn
- Designing an onboarding process for new customers
- Implementing loyalty programs
- Establishes feedback system
- Designs upselling/cross-selling campaigns
- Measuring customer satisfaction and lifetime value"

Digital marketing

Content Marketing: "Create Content Marketing Plan for [Industry]:

- Topic calendar based on seasonal trends
- Content formats for different channels
- SEO optimization and keyword strategy
- Marketing and other collaborations
- Performance measurement and analysis
- Reuse and repurpose of content"

Social media strategy: "Develop a social media strategy that:

- Defines presence on relevant platforms
- Creates platform-specific content
- Establishes community management routines
- Implementing social media analytics
- Integration with other marketing channels
- Measures engagement and conversion"

18. Using prompts for education and training

Educational prompts are designed to facilitate learning, knowledge transfer, and skill development. These prompts must be adapted to different learning styles, proficiency levels, and educational goals.

Pedagogical structuring

Course design: "Create a structured course on [topic] for [target audience]:

- Learning objectives and competence objectives
- Module division with logical progression
- Theoretical concepts and practical applications
- Exercises and assignments for each module
- Assessment criteria and examination forms
- Resources and literature references"

Lesson planning: "Develop a detailed lesson plan for [topic]:

- Introduction that arouses interest
- Step-by-step review of the material
- Interactive elements and discussion questions
- Practical examples and case studies
- Summary and reflection
- Follow-up activities for in-depth study"

Adaptive teaching

Differentiated Instruction: "Create instructional materials for [subject] that:

- Adaptable for different learning styles (visual, auditory, kinesthetic)
- Provides different difficulty levels
- Includes support materials for students with needs
- Offers challenges for advanced students
- Integrates technology and digital tools
- Enables self-study and independent learning"

Formative assessment: "Design assessment tools that:

- Measures understanding during the learning process
- Provides immediate feedback to students
- Identifies knowledge gaps early
- Adapt teaching based on results
- Documenting learning progress
- Motivates continued commitment"

Professional development

Skill training: "Develop training programs for [skill]:

- Basic theoretical background
- Practical exercises with gradual difficulty
- Simulations of real-life situations
- Feedback mechanisms and self-evaluation
- Guidance and peer learning
- Continuous development and follow-up"

Leadership training: "Create leadership training that:

- Develops self-awareness and emotional intelligence
- Trains communication and conflict resolution
- Builds team leadership and delegation skills
- Includes strategic thinking and decision-making
- Addresses ethics and accountability
- Enables practical application in the work role"

19. Evaluating and improving prompts

Prompt evaluation is a systematic process for measuring effectiveness, identifying areas for improvement, and optimizing outcomes. This requires structured methods for assessing quality, relevance, and usability.

Evaluation criteria

Qualitative metrics: "Evaluate prompt performance based on:

- Relevance to original question
- Factual accuracy and credibility
- Clarity and comprehensibility for the target audience
- Completeness of information
- Structure and logical organization
- Creativity and originality when relevant"

Quantitative metrics: "Measure prompt effectiveness by:

- Time to generate acceptable response
- The number of iterations required for the desired result
- Proportion of responses used without modification
- User satisfaction on a scale of 1-10
- Conversion rate for business-related prompts
- Engagement and interaction for content prompts"

Iterative improvement

A/B testing: "Implement systematic testing of prompts:

- Create variations of the same prompt with different approaches
- Test on a representative sample of users
- Document the performance of each variant
- Analyze statistical significance of differences
- Implement the most effective version
- Keep iterating based on new insights"

Feedback integration: "Establish systems for continuous improvement:

- Collect user feedback systematically
- Identify recurring problems and limitations
- Analyze failed prompts for lessons learned
- Update prompt library with improvements
- Document proven methods and pitfalls
- Train teams in improved techniques"

Performance optimization

Efficiency Analysis: "Optimize prompt performance by:

- Identification of unnecessary elements that can be removed
- Clarification of unclear instructions
- Balancing specificity and flexibility
- Adapting tone and style for the target audience
- Integration of contextual information
- Testing different structural approaches"

Scalability: "Develop prompts for large-scale use:

- Standardization of format and structure
- Automation of continuous elements
- Adaptation for different user groups
- Integration with existing workflows and systems
- Documentation for easy implementation
- Training users in effective application"

20. Prompt Writing Tools and Resources

A rich ecosystem of tools and resources is available to support prompt development, testing, and optimization. These tools range from plain text editors to sophisticated AI-assisted platforms.

Developer tools

Prompt editors: Specialized text editors with features such as syntax highlighting for prompt structures, templates for common prompt types, versioning for prompt iterations (improvement cycles), collaborative editing features, and integration with AI models for live testing.

Testing platforms: Platforms that enable systematic testing of prompts with features such as batch testing of multiple prompts, A/B testing with statistical analysis, performance metrics and benchmarking, user feedback integration, and automated report generation.

Analysis tools

Prompt Analysis: Tools that analyze prompt quality by evaluating clarity and specificity, identifying potential ambiguities, suggesting improvements and optimizations, measuring complexity and readability, and comparing them to best standards.

Performance Monitoring: Systems that track prompt performance over time through metrics such as response time and quality, user engagement and satisfaction, business prompt conversion rates, error reports and diagnostics, and usage trends and patterns.

Resources and community

Documentation: Extensive resources include official documentation for AI models, prompt technology guides and tutorials, collections of best practices, common issues and solutions, and regular updates on new features.

Community Platforms: Active communities provide prompting technology discussion forums, sharing successful prompts and techniques, peer review and feedback, collaborative projects and initiatives, and networking opportunities with experts.

Specialized tools

Industry-specific solutions: Tools tailored for specific domains include legal prompt generators, medical and scientific templates, business and marketing tools, education and training resources, and technical documentation tools.

Automation: Advanced systems offer automatic prompt generation based on goals, dynamic adaptation based on feedback, integration with workflow systems, scheduled execution and reporting, and application programming interfaces (APIs) for custom integration.

21. The future of prompt design and AI interaction

The development of prompt design follows technological advances in artificial intelligence and changing user needs. These developments affect both how we interact with AI systems and the possibilities they open for creative and professional applications.

Technological trends

Contextual intelligence: Future AI systems will have improved ability to understand and use context from past interactions, external data sources, and user profiles, enabling more personalized and relevant responses without requiring users to repeat background information.

Multimodal integration: The trend is towards AI systems that can process and integrate text, images, audio, and other data into the same prompt. This opens richer and more nuanced forms of communication where users can combine diverse types of input for more precise results.

User experience

Interactivity: Future prompt designs are expected to be more conversational and natural. This means that AI systems will be able to follow up on questions, request clarification, and suggest alternative courses of action without the user having to provide explicit instructions.

Adaptive personalization: AI systems will learn individual users' communication styles, preferences, and needs over time, automatically adapting prompt interpretation and response formats for optimal user experience.

Professional application

Automated prompt optimization: Machine learning will be used to automatically improve prompts based on usage and results, reducing the need for manual optimization and making effective prompts available to more users.

Domain specialization: The trend is towards highly specialized AI assistants for specific industries and use cases, with built-in understanding of domain-specific terminology, processes, and requirements.

Ethical considerations

Transparency and explainability: Future systems will offer greater visibility into how prompts are interpreted and processed, enabling greater trust and more informed use of AI assistants.

Bias management: Development focuses on identifying and reducing bias in prompt interpretation and response generation, ensuring more fair and inclusive AI interactions.

22. Case studies and examples

Practical case studies demonstrate how effective prompts are applied in real-world situations and illustrate the principles of successful prompt design in different contexts.

Technical documentation

Case study: A software company needed to generate API documentation for a complex system with hundreds of endpoints.

Challenge: Manual documentation was time-consuming and often incomplete or outdated.

Prompt solution: "Analyze the following API code and generate complete documentation that includes endpoint description, parameters with data types and validation, response formats and examples, error codes and handling, authentication requirements, and usage examples for common scenarios."

Result: Documentation time was reduced by 70% while quality and consistency were significantly improved.

Customer service

Case study: An e-commerce company wanted to automate first-line customer service for frequent questions.

Challenge: Customers asked related questions about deliveries, returns, and product information, but with variations in wording and context.

Prompt Solution: "Based on the following customer question: [customer message], provide a helpful, professional response that includes specific information from our knowledge base, relevant policies, and next steps for the customer. If the question requires personal assistance, kindly escalate to a human agent."

Result: 60% of customer requests could be managed automatically with high customer satisfaction.

Educational content

Case Study: A university needed to create engaging online course materials for distance learning students.

Challenge: Traditional course materials were too static and did not engage students in the online environment.

Prompt Solution: "Create interactive course materials for [topic] that include engaging introductions, practical examples from real-world situations, reflection questions for discussion, activities that apply knowledge, and summaries that reinforce key concepts."

Results: Student engagement increased by 40% and course implementation improved significantly.

Creative content production

Case study: A marketing agency needed to produce substantial amounts of customized content for different clients and channels.

Challenge: Each client had unique brand guidelines, target audiences, and communication styles.

Prompt Solution: "Create [content type] for [brand] that follows their brand personality [description], targets [target audience], and achieves the goal of [specific goal]. The content should be [tone and style] and include [specific elements]."

Result: Content production time was reduced by 50% while maintaining quality and brand consistency.

23. Summary and key points

Effective prompt design is a skill that combines technical understanding, creative communication, and strategic thinking. This guide has presented comprehensive principles and practical techniques for maximizing the results of AI interactions.

Basic principles

Clarity is fundamental to any successful prompt design. Specific instructions produce better results than vague requests. Context helps AI systems understand the intended application and tailor responses accordingly. Structure in prompt construction facilitates processing and improves the quality of results.

Strategic application

Diverse types of tasks require different prompting strategies. Creative tasks benefit from open-ended, inspiring prompts, while technical tasks require precision and detailed specifications. Business-related prompts must balance creativity with strategic goals and measurable results.

Continuous improvement

Prompt development is an iterative (continuous) process that requires systematic evaluation and improvement. Testing different approaches, collecting feedback, and analyzing results are essential to developing truly effective prompts. Documenting successful techniques builds organizational knowledge and expertise.

Future perspectives

Advances in AI technology will continue to change how we interact with intelligent systems. Understanding basic prompting principles will remain relevant even as technology evolves, as effective communication will always be central to successful AI interactions.

24. Frequently Asked Questions (FAQ)

How long should a prompt be?

There is no absolute rule for prompt length, but effectiveness is more important than scope. Short, specific prompts often work better than long, complex instructions. Include all necessary information but avoid redundancy. For complex tasks, longer prompts may be necessary, but structure them clearly with headings and bullet points.

What do I do if the AI doesn't understand my prompt?

Rephrase your request using simpler language and a clearer structure. Break complex tasks into smaller parts. Provide concrete examples of what you want to achieve. Specify the format and style of the response. Make sure you have included all the necessary contextual information.

How can I get more creative answers?

Encourage creativity by asking for alternative approaches or perspectives. Use open-ended questions instead of closed ones. Ask for brainstorming or innovative solutions. Specify that you welcome unusual or experimental ideas. Combine different domains or perspectives in your request.

Can I reuse successful prompts?

Yes, successful prompts can and should be reused and adapted for similar situations. Create templates based on prompts that work well. Document effective wording and structures. Adapt the basic structure for different contexts and audiences. Build a library of proven prompting techniques.

How do I ensure quality in AI-generated content?

Always review AI-generated content for factual accuracy and relevance. Use AI as a tool for first drafts, not as a final product. Combine AI-generated content with human expertise and judgment. Implement quality control processes for important content. Validate claims and references from independent sources.

What are the most common mistakes in prompt design?

Overly vague instructions lead to unclear results. Lack of context makes it difficult for AI to understand intent. Overly complicated prompts can confuse more than they help. Forgetting to specify the format and style of the response. Not testing and iterating prompts for improvement. Expecting perfect results without revision.

How do I deal with bias in AI responses?

Be aware that AI systems may reflect bias from training data. Ask follow-up questions from different perspectives. Ask for alternative perspectives on sensitive topics. Critically review responses for potential bias. Use diverse sources for verification. Encourage inclusive and balanced perspectives in your prompts.

25. Conclusion and further reading

Prompt design represents a new form of communication that is becoming increasingly important in our AI-driven world. Mastering this skill opens opportunities for more efficient work processes, more creative problem solving, and more productive interactions with intelligent systems.

Important lessons learned

Effective prompt design is based on an understanding of both technical capabilities and human communication principles. Success requires practice, experimentation, and continuous improvement. No prompt is perfect from the start, but systematic development and application of proven principles lead to noticeable improvement in results.

Practical application

Start with simple prompts and gradually develop more sophisticated techniques. Document successful approaches for future use. Experiment with unique styles and structures to find what works best for your specific needs. Share experiences with colleagues and learn from the successes and mistakes of others.

Skills development

Prompt design is a skill that develops over time through practical applications. Stay up to date on new AI features and techniques. Engage in networks and conversations around prompt optimization. Experiment with new techniques and approaches regularly. Reflect on your experiences and learn from both successes and failures.

Future opportunities

AI technology is evolving rapidly and will offer new opportunities for creative and productive use. Basic prompt design skills will remain valuable even as technology evolves. Investing in understanding and mastering these techniques will yield long-term benefits in both professional and personal contexts.

Effective prompt design is both an art and a science that combines creativity with a systematic approach. By applying the principles and techniques in this guide, users can develop their skills and achieve better results in their AI interactions. The future belongs to those who can communicate effectively with intelligent systems, and prompt design is the key to this communication.